Günter Gerngross
Herbert Puchta

Join us for English

1

Pupil's Book

Contents

1 Welcome back!

1 Listen and sing. Hello again!

2 Listen, point and repeat.

3 Listen and stick (page 73).

4 Listen and say the chant.

The tiger jump,
The tiger jump,

Come on, let's do
The tiger jump.

one two three four five

six seven eight nine ten

1 Welcome back!

5 Listen and stick (page 73).

Check your English!

1 Stick in your photo.

2 Read and answer.

....

....

....

....

My progress

2 In the classroom

1 Listen and point. Speak.

2  **Listen and say the chant.**

One, two, three, four, five, six, seven, eight, nine, ten, and now eleven.

Twelve is two plus ten. Now let's start again.

3 **Read and colour the frames.**

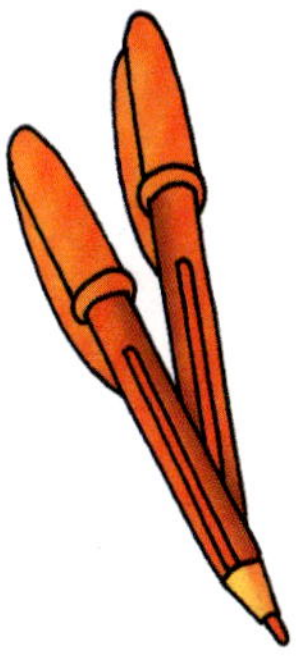

two pens

five rulers

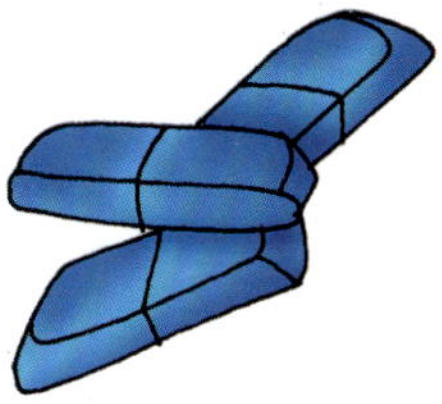

four pencils

one pencil case

three rubbers

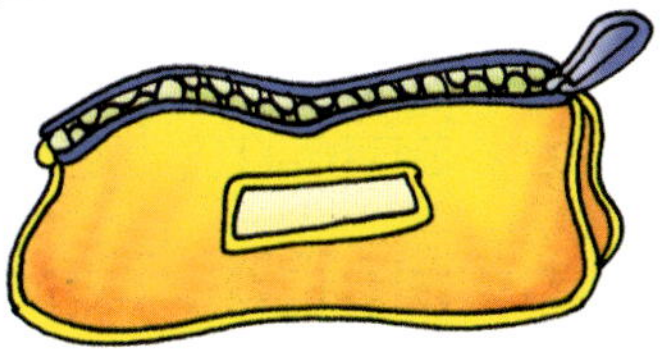

4 Play the game.

5 Count and write the numbers.

How many red bags? ....five..........

How many orange pencils? ....

How many blue and yellow rubbers? ....

How many pink and green pens? ....

6 Listen and write the numbers.

_ _ _ _ _ _ _

_ _ _ _ _ _ _

_ _ _ _ _ _ _

....

2 In the classroom

7 Listen and mime.

8 Listen and write the numbers.

Check your English!

1 Look and write.

2 Read and tick.

My progress

3 Colours

1 Listen, point and repeat.

2 Read and write the numbers.

(4) blue	( ) pink	( ) brown
( ) red	( ) green	( ) black
( ) orange	( ) yellow	( ) white

3 Listen and sing. The butterfly

4 Listen and stick (page 73) - Magic milk.

5 Listen and colour.

6 Listen and mime.

7 Listen and write the numbers.

Check your English!

1 Colour and write.

A pink ....

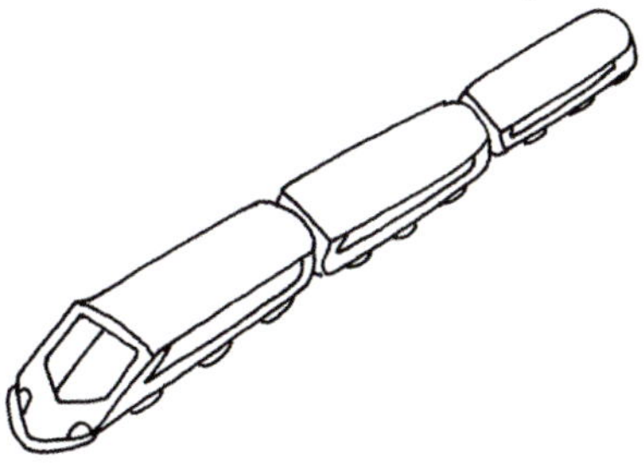

A green ....

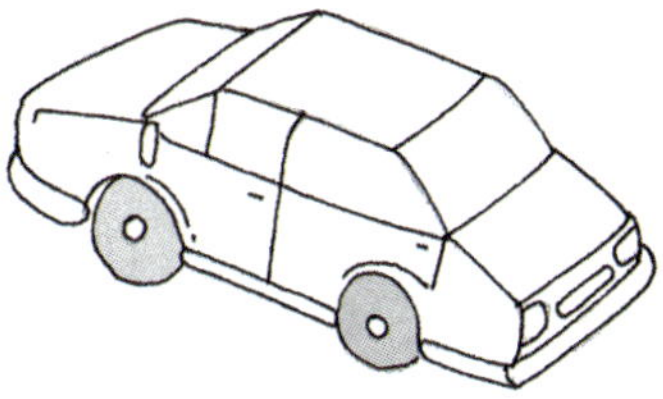

An orange ....

A blue ....

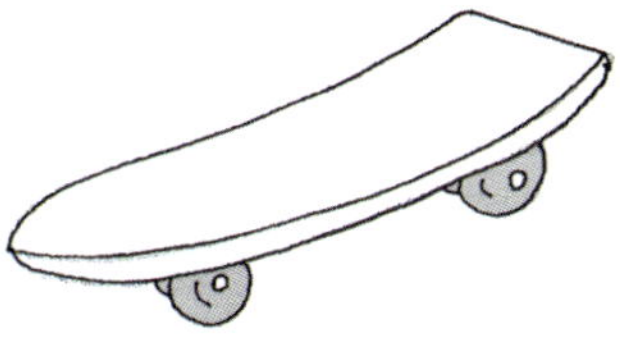

A yellow ....

A brown ....

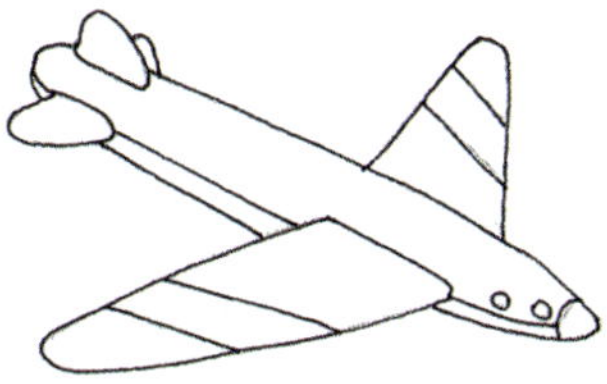

A red and yellow ....

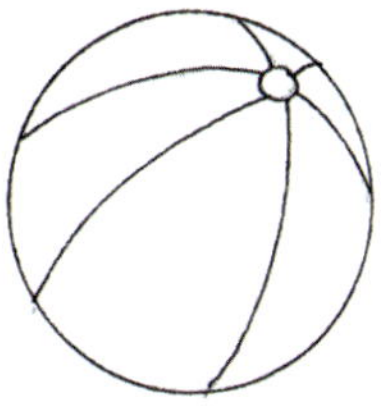

A black and white ....

My progress

Books, bo

This is a library. Lots of people come here to read books.

Read and match.

My book is excellent. It´s a story about three monsters. The monsters are green, yellow, blue, white and orange.

My book is blue It´s a story about two animals. One is very big and one is very small It´s great!

Look! My book is yellow In the picture there´s a brown, blue and white boat.

My book is very good. It´s a story about my favourite sport. In the picture there´s a ball. It´s white, red and blue.

oks, books

1

2

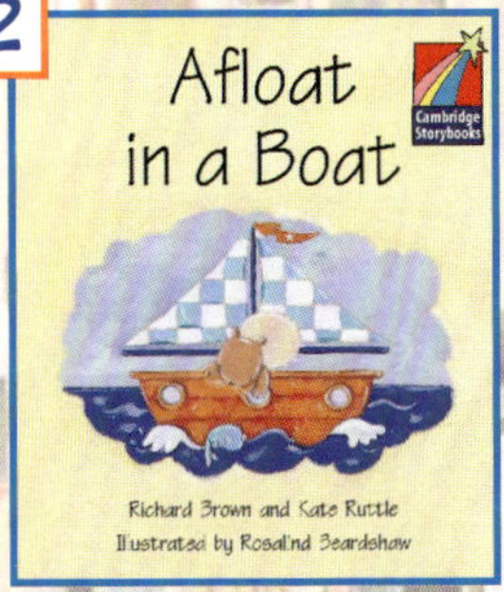

3

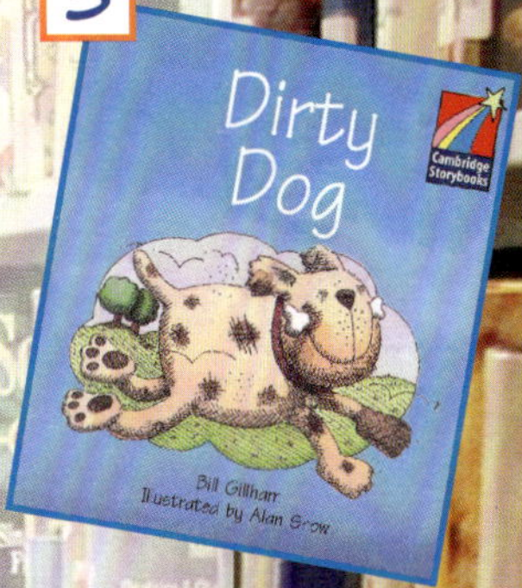

4

5

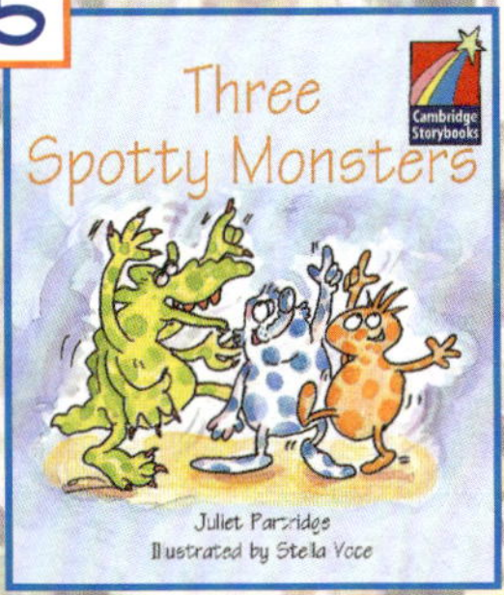

6

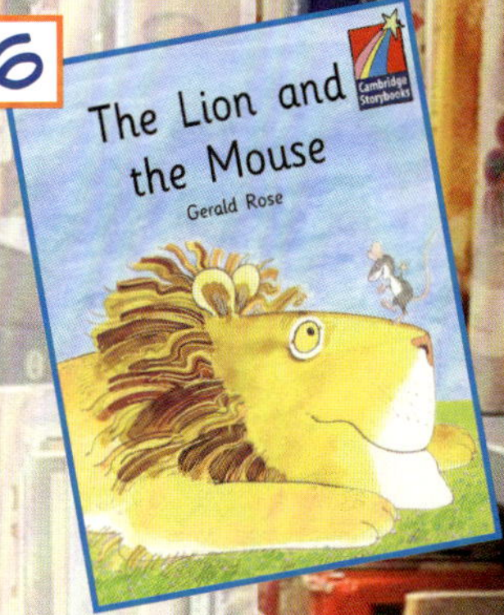

7

8

My favourite book is

....

....

....

4 My house

1 Listen, point and repeat.

2 Listen and say the chant.

3 Listen and mime.

4 Listen and write the numbers.

5 Listen and stick (page 75) - Where's Magic?

He´s not here.
Dad, where´s Magic?
He´s in your bedroom.
Izzy, wizzy, hey, hey, hey! Bed, go away!
He´s under the bed. Thank you!
Zzz

6 Listen and write the numbers.

☐  ☐  ☐ 

7 Play the game (Mini flashcards - Magic - page 69).

Check your English!

1 Read and stick (page 75).

garden　　living room　　kitchen

bedroom　　bathroom

2 Tick.

☐ on	☐ under	☐ under
☐ in	☐ on	☐ in

My progress

5 A B C, food for me!

1 Listen, point and repeat.

2 Speak.

3 Listen and point.

ABCD
Come with me.
EFG
Let's have some tea.
HIJK
It's my birthday!
LMNOP
A party for you and me.
QRSTU
Here's a party hat for you.
VWXYZ
My party hat is on my head.

4 Listen and sing. *The alphabet song*

5 Complete the alphabet.

6 Listen and mime.

7 Listen and write the numbers.

8 Listen and write the numbers.

9 What letters are missing? Say, listen and check.

_HI_S _ANA_AS

APP__S CH_C_EN

SAN__ICHES E_GS

C_EE_E C_KES

__ANGE __ICE

Check your English!

1 Read and stick (page 75).

apples	bananas	sandwiches	chips
cakes	eggs	chicken	cheese

2 Find the words and write.

EGGSCHEESECAKESANDWICHESORANGEJUICECHICKENAPPLES

....

....

....

My progress

6 Clothes

1 Listen, point and repeat.

2 Listen and colour.

3 Listen and sing.

Toby and Tina's new clothes

Look at Tina, look at Tina,
Oh, this can't be true,
She's wearing orange socks and a blue hat too,
She's wearing a lovely pink skirt,
And a green and yellow T-shirt!

Hey Tina, you're so cool,
You're cool, cool, cool!
Hey, Tina you're so cool!

Look at Toby, look at Toby,
Oh, this can't be true!
He's wearing yellow jeans just for you,
He's wearing a pink and yellow shoe,
He's like a parrot in a zoo!

Hey Toby, you're so cool,
You're cool, cool, cool!
Hey, Toby you're so cool!

4 Colour.

6 Clothes

5 Listen and stick (page 73) - Funny cat!

Sorry, I don´t know.
Look at Magic!
Oh no!
What a funny cat!

6 Listen and mime.

7 Listen and write the numbers.

Check your English!

1 Read and stick (page 73).

skirt jeans shoes

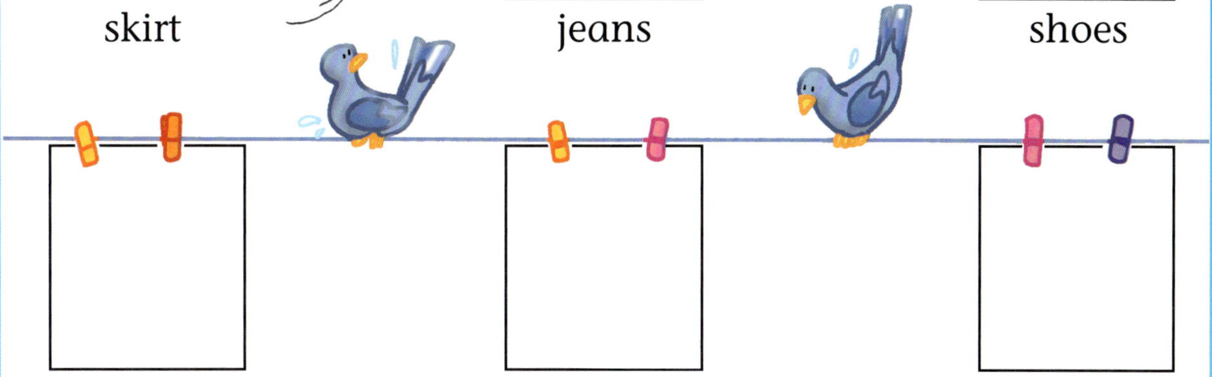

sweater T-shirt socks

2 Colour and write.

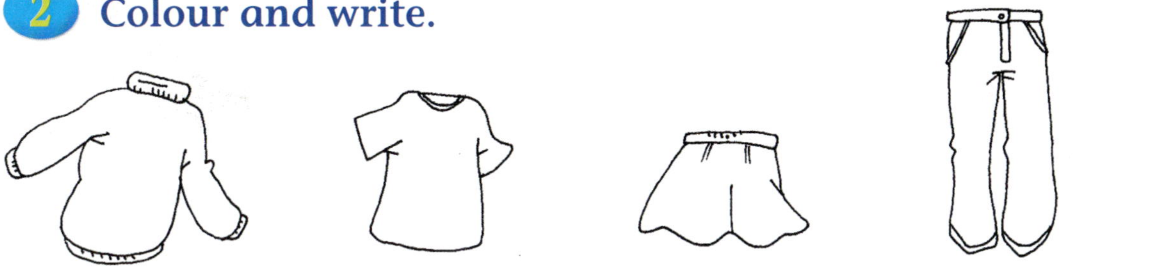

....

....

My progress

School Uniforms

Children at school in Great Britain wear school uniforms.
Look and match.

1

2

A

Look at my school uniform.
White T-shirt, grey shorts,
grey socks and black shoes.

C

I don't like
my school uniform!
Blue blazer, white shirt,
yellow and blue tie,
grey trousers and
black shoes.

B

This is a photo
of me and Paul.
Do you like my
new school uniform?
White shirt, black,
red and white tie,
black and red blazer.

D

At school I wear a uniform:
a red sweater, a red tie,
a blue skirt,
a white shirt, white socks
and black shoes.

7 At the circus

1 Listen, point and repeat.

2 Listen and sing.

Twenty little monkeys

Twenty little monkeys are jumping on the bed.
One falls off and bumps his head.

Nineteen... Eighteen... Seventeen...
Sixteen... Fifteen... Fourteen...
Thirteen... Twelve... Eleven...

Ten little monkeys are jumping on the bed.
They all fall off and bump their head.

3 Listen and stick (page 73) - The lion.

4 Do the sums. Colour the picture.

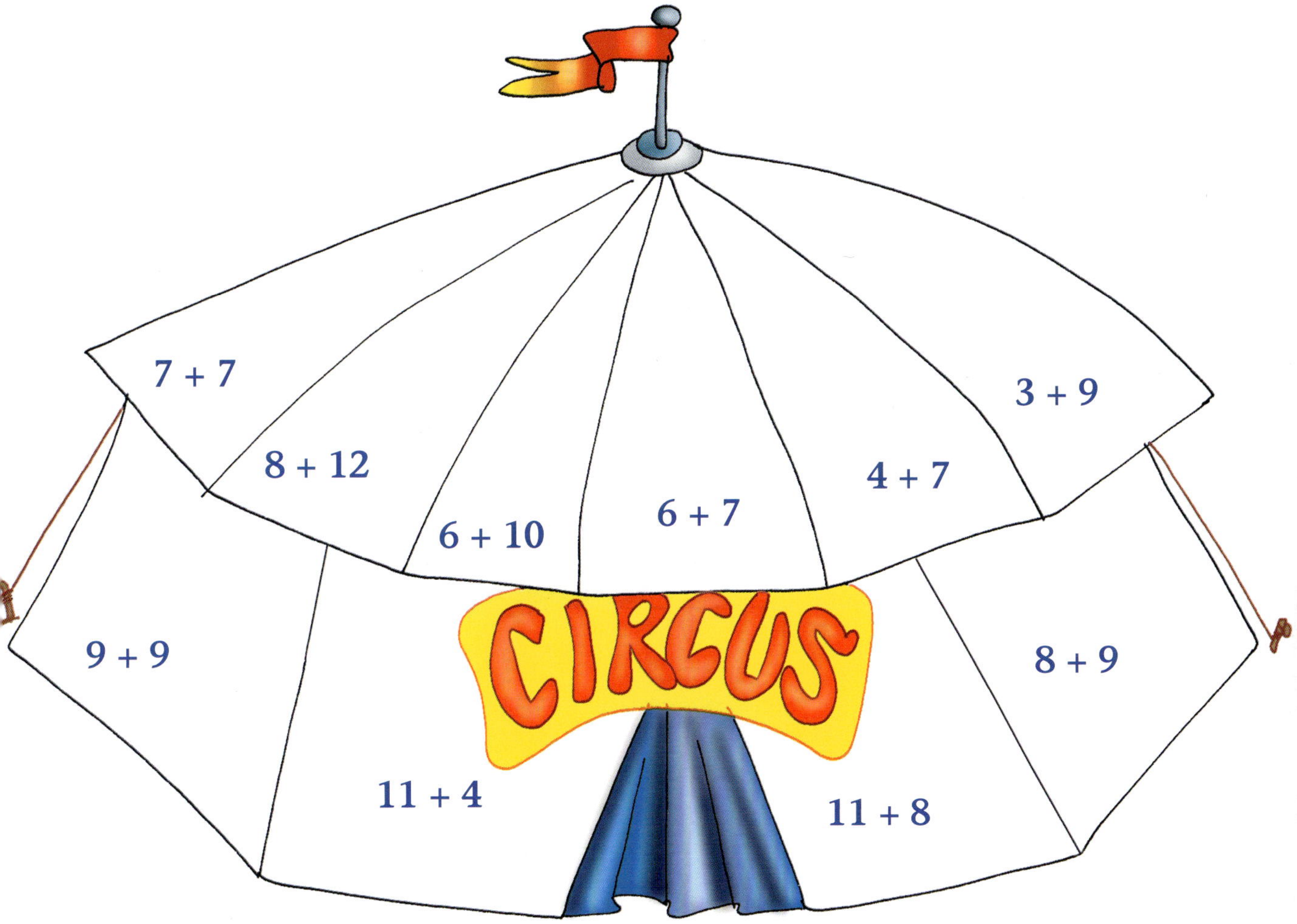

eleven
twelve
thirteen
fourteen
fifteen
sixteen
seventeen
eighteen
nineteen
twenty

7 At the circus

5 Play the game.

6 Play Bingo.

Check your English!

1 Read and stick (page 73). 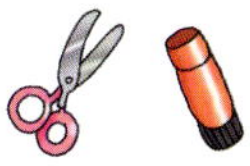

eleven	twelve	thirteen	fourteen	fifteen
sixteen	seventeen	eighteen	nineteen	twenty

2 Do the sums.

7 + 4 = ...eleven.... 9 + 3 = ...

2 + 16 = ... 6 + 7 = ...

3 + 17 = ... 8 + 8 = ...

My progress

8 Pets

1 Listen, point and repeat.

Have you got a pet?
Yes, I have.
What have you got?
I've got a cat and a mouse,
a rabbit and a dog,
a budgie, a fish and a frog.

2 Listen and say the chant.

3  Listen and tick.

4 Tick true or false.

		T	F
1	Julia's cat is black and white.		
2	Steve's budgie is blue and white.		
3	Jeff's mouse is brown.		
4	Maria's rabbit is brown and white.		

5 Listen and stick (page 75) - Mike's pets.

Squeak! Squeak!
Have you got a mouse?
Where is it?
I don't know.
Aaaaggghhh!
?
Uh-oh. It's my mum!
Hee, hee, hee!
Mike, look!
Sorry, Mum.

6 Listen and mime.

7 Listen and write the numbers.

Check your English!

1 Read and stick (page 75). 

cat | fish | rabbit | frog

dog | mouse | budgie

2 Write and colour.

a blue ....

a black ....

a brown ....

a green and red

....

My progress

9 A birthday party

1 Listen, point and repeat.

When's Pit's birthday?
In January, February
or March?
No, no, no.
In April, May or June?
No, no, no.
In July, August
or September?
No, no, no.
In October or November?
No! Please remember:
It's in December!

2 Listen and say the birthday chant.

3 Listen and tick.

- [ ] April
- [x] November
- [x] 8
- [ ] 10

- [ ] June
- [ ] October
- [ ] 9
- [ ] 10

- [ ] March
- [ ] May
- [ ] 11
- [ ] 12

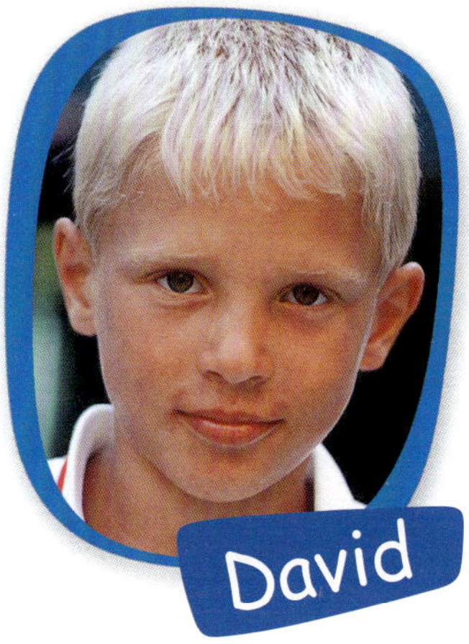

- [ ] September
- [ ] December
- [ ] 9
- [ ] 10

4 Make a chart for your class birthdays.

January		July	
February		August	
March		September	
April		October	
May		November	
June	Paul	December	

5 Listen and stick (page 75) - A birthday cake for Pit.

And here´s your cake.
HAPPY BIRTHDAY
What a big cake! Thanks!
Oh dear!
HAPPY BIRTHDAY
HAPPY BIRTHDAY
WHAM!
My lovely cake!

9 A birthday party

6 Listen and mime.

7 Listen and write the numbers.

Check your English!

1 Write the months.

January .... March .... May .... July

.... September .... November ....

2 Match.

1 When's your birthday?	Thank you!
2 Let's make a cake.	Eight.
3 Here's your present.	In November.
4 How old are you?	Good idea!

3 Complete the text.

nine - birthday - party - June

I'm Sandra. I'm ....

My .... is in .... I have my ....

in the garden.

My progress

Happy

Today is
Sam's birthday.
Let's go to
his party.

my birthday cake

I'm having a party
with my friends.
At my party I've got balloons
and lots of party food:
chocolate biscuits,
marshmallows and lots more!
Look at my cake!
Do you like cakes?
Happy
birthday!
crisps
chocolate biscuits
marshmallows

Birthday!

my party invitation

my birthday cards

a party hat

party bags

balloons

party food

a party popper

Christmas

1 Listen and sing. Merry Christmas

We wish you a Merry Christmas,
We wish you a Merry Christmas,
We wish you a Merry Christmas,
And a Happy New Year!

2 Colour and write.

From ....

3 Make a Christmas card.

Easter

1 Colour and cut.

2 Make an Easter card.

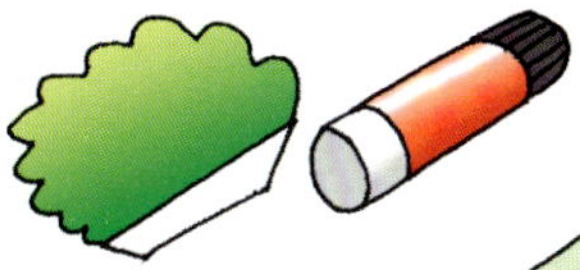

Mini flashcards

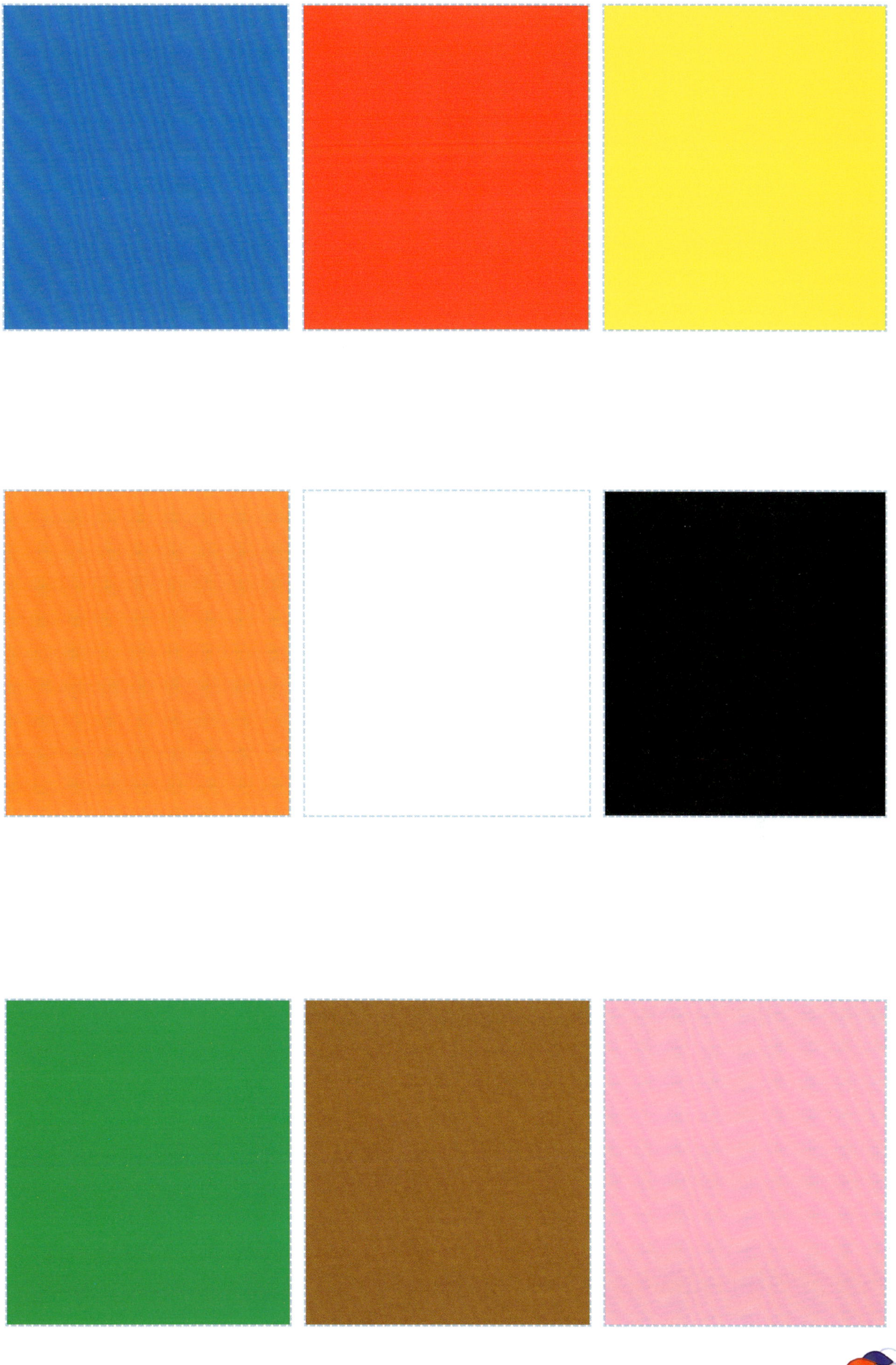

Mini flashcards

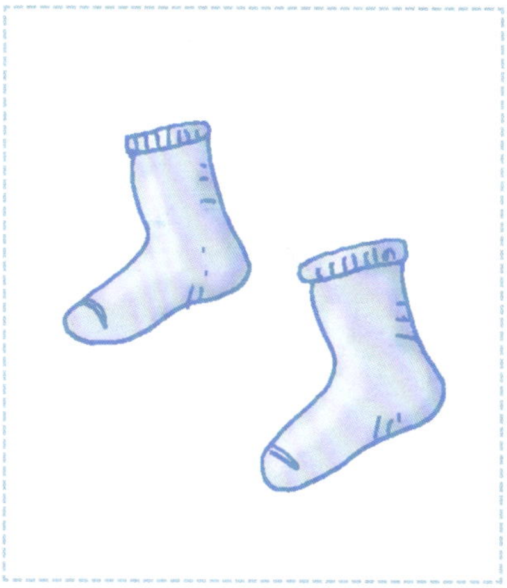

Mini flashcards

p. 4

Rita | Nick | Rob | Lisa

p. 6

Hello. | What's your name? | Paul.

p. 39

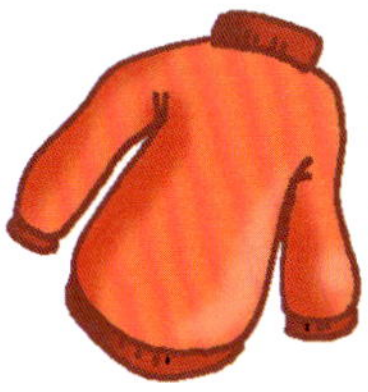

p. 44

I've got an idea.

Jump!

Come back!

p. 18

p. 36/37

Where's my pink sweater?

Where are my green shoes?

Where's my red T-shirt?

Where are my blue jeans?

p. 47

p. 24/25

Look in the garden.

Look in the kitchen.

Look in the living room.

Look in the bathroom.

p. 27

p. 33

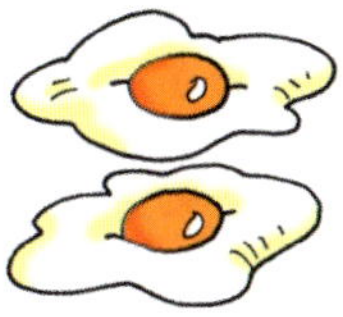

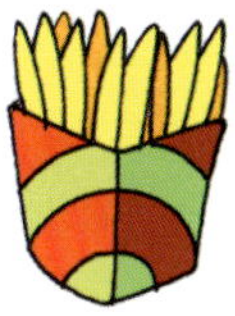

p. 50/51

Have you got a dog?

Thank you, Mike!

Yes, I have.

p. 53

p. 56/57

You're welcome.

Quick! Let's run into the house.

Happy birthday!

Wordlist

Unit 1 - Welcome back!
Hooray!
one
two
three
four
five
six
seven
eight
nine
ten
lion
frog
crocodile
cat
elephant
mouse
Hello!
Hi!
What's your name?
How old are you?
I'm eight.
Bye-bye!

Unit 2 - In the classroom
pencil case
book
bag
pen
pencil
rubber
ruler
How are you?
I'm OK.
I'm fine thank you.
How many?
What's your phone number?
My phone number is 521 689.
caterpillar

Unit 3 - Colours
blue
red
orange
pink
green
yellow
brown
black
white
butterfly
milk
bike
ball
boat
train
plane
doll
skateboard
Throw the ball.
Look up.
Ouch!

Unit 4 - My house
bedroom
bathroom
living room
kitchen
garden
bed
table
chair
cupboard
watch
Where's Magic?
He's not here.
in
on
under

Unit 5 - A B C, food for me!
sandwich
cake
orange juice
apple
chicken
cheese
banana
chips

eggs
Do you like chicken?
Yes, I do. / No, I don't.

Unit 6 - Clothes

sweater
skirt
jeans
socks
shoes
T-shirt
hat
parrot
She's wearing orange socks.
He's wearing yellow jeans.
Where's my red T-shirt?
Sorry, I don't know.
Put on your jeans.
Look for your shoes.
tie
blazer
shirt
trousers

Unit 7 - At the circus

eleven
twelve
thirteen
fourteen
fifteen
sixteen
seventeen
eighteen
nineteen
twenty
monkey
What's the number?

Unit 8 - Pets

Have you got a pet? Yes, I have.
What have you got?
I've got a cat.
What colour is it?
budgie
cat
mouse
dog
rabbit
fish
Come in.
Where is it?
Sorry, Mum!

Unit 9 - A birthday party

January
February
March
April
May
June
July
August
September
October
November
December
When's Pit's birthday?
Please remember.
calendar
presents
candles
birthday cake
birthday card
Today is Pit's birthday.
Happy birthday!
Let's make a cake.
What a big cake!
Good idea.
Quick!
Oh dear!
Open your present.
Cut the cake.
party invitation
party bag
party popper
crisps
chocolate biscuits
marshmallows
party food

DIPLOMA

This is to certify that

....

....

has completed
Level 1 of JOIN US

School ....

Teacher ....

Date ....